Rampant Inertia

Also by Alan Halsey

Auto Dada Café
Five Years Out 1982-1987
The Text of Shelley's Death
A Robin Hood Book
Wittgenstein's Devil: Selected Writing 1978-1998
Marginalien: Poems, Prose & Graphics 1988-2004
Not Everything Remotely: Selected Poems 1978-2005
Lives of the Poets
Term as in Aftermath
Even If Only Out Of
In White Writing

Alan Halsey

Rampant Inertia

Shearsman Books

First published in the United Kingdom in 2014 by
Shearsman Books
50 Westons Hill Drive
Emersons Green
BRISTOL
BS16 7DF

Shearsman Books Ltd Registered Office
30–31 St. James Place, Mangotsfield, Bristol BS16 9JB
(this address not for correspondence)

www.shearsman.com

ISBN 978-1-84861-356-0

Copyright © Alan Halsey, 2014.
The right of Alan Halsey to be identified as the author
of this work has been asserted by him in accordance with the
Copyrights, Designs and Patents Act of 1988.
All rights reserved.

ACKNOWLEDGEMENTS

Some of these poems first appeared in *This Corner: Blue Issue*, *A Sheffield Anthology*, *e.ratio*, *A Mutual Friend: Poems for Charles Dickens* (Two Rivers 2012), *Blart*, *Breakthrough Nostalgia: Reading Steve McCaffery Then and Now* (*Open Letter* 14.7), *Listening to the Night: Tower of Babel Poems* (Like This 2013), *The Other Room Anthology 4*, *Golden Handcuffs Review*, *Black Box Manifold*, *Free Poetry*, *Gathered Here Today: Celebrating Geraldine Monk at 60* (Knives Forks & Spoons 2012) and *Antiphon*.

Cover drawings from the author's *Transcriptions Pending Translation*,
copyright © Alan Halsey, 2014.

Contents

Austerity Stuffing

Rampant Inertia	9
Black Hawk Island 21 Oct 2010	10
England in 1836: A Digest	12
Letter to Timothy Donnelly dated 2 a.m. 26 Dec 2011	17
Amongst	18
Mutability Cento:	
a Sheffield cacophony for 10 or more voices	20
Nothing by Nobody:	
An Interrupted Reading of Burton's *Anatomy*, 2011	25
All Told	29
Les Hiboux, or the 19th Century & After	31
Austerity Sonnet	32
In Their Manner of Speaking: Directions Towards	
a Performance in Mime of *Our Mutual Friend*	33
Frugal Fractals	36
In an Annex of the Gallery at the End of Time	40
Austerity Stuffing	42

Cachemphaton

Northland Macaronic	49
From the Horse's Mouth:	
A Transcript & Homage to Dr Swift	50
Le Testament de Mr Pepys	52
H.C. Earwicker's Train Ride	55
The Clinamen Transfigured	58
Cachemphaton	65
An Internet Sieve for Aretino's Positions	66
Poem Written in Babel, May 2012	69
Sound Poems for Performance with Mick Beck	71
Lewis & Clark: An Imaginary Conversation	74

The Return of the Logoclast

Safe Passage	79
Those Troublesome Disguises of	
Jonathan Williams in Bartram's Tree	81
Sixty Dyads for David Annwn	85
Local Forum	87
On St Martin's Land:	
William of Newburgh Annotates a Poem by J.H. Prynne	89
Plot Likelihoods	90
Idle Time Scans	98
She didn't need to keep birds	106
The Return of the Logoclast	107
LOXHD1	108
Complexicon	109
Searching for Sibylla	111
Messenger, Singer	112
A Defence of Poetry	113
Rampant Inertia Revisited: A Busted Sonnet	114

Austerity Stuffing

Rampant Inertia

precis : debris

& down by the logos gardens
edible bibles, sleepless lexicons
difficult decisions which suddenly
pronounced the ordure of the day
scorpion acorns in ivied boast
now nobody's got time or change
for oxymorons of Homeric voltage
rarer than rhyme in boardrooms
where jobbers in belljars
the word is probably 'jabber'
but now that's off my chest

cachemphaton
foul speech

'The sowe sate on hi benche
and harpydde Robyn Hoode'

while the translation in anagrams
of *Aeneid* Book One stalled at
A ram, quiver moan, jot a cure or as I quip

despite pinchbeck chokepears
household versifiers
wiredrawn paranymphs
& sundry other unsolved clues
to the Mystery of A.C. Swinburne

'the Time has passed away'
John Taylor wrote to Clare
'in which Poetry will answer'

Black Hawk Island 23 Oct 2010

for Michael Mann

in exchange for haiku
    back at Lorine's
        leopard frogs

a dozen
    hundreds
        a thousand!

heading for
    with one last jump
        Rock River

*

where the hell's that
    poem about her
        broken-down pump

did I dream it?
    at least I have a
        photo –

of the pump,
    not
        the poem

*

    'weed trees' grown up
       where friend tree
          used to be

and the cabin
     Ann tells me
       is as was

not the sofa
     where my wife & friend
        sit comfy

England in 1836: A Digest

(edited from Najaf Koolee Meerza
Journal of a Residence in England, trans. Assaad Y. Kayat)

1. A garden heaven
adorned with roses of different colours in every direction
the water was running on the beautiful green
pictures were drawn on every wall.
Here and there were young moonly faces selling refreshments.
There were burning in this place about two millions
of lanterns and lights arranged to make poetry
in such manner that they have no end.

2. 10,000 Frank moons*
*English ladies
walking and gazing about where the roses and their tribes
were admiring their beautiful cheeks.
Each was taken by the hand
such a company in such a place says to the soul
Behold thy paradise
every one asked for a glass of refreshment
to present to the possessors of jasmine hands.

3. The learned men of England have dug a tunnel
the construction of which would never enter the human mind.
They have most wonderfully succeeded
in making a road under the river Thames
miraculously lighted and free of all damp
it may be called a glory of the country
the ships pass over the heads of the people.

4. By geometrical wisdom they have made a box of iron
in which they put water to boil. Underneath
is like an urn and from it when the steam rises up
the wheels take their motion

the coach spreads its wings
and the travellers become like birds.

5. What a number of most valuable jewels!
What a quantity of gold vessels! On our way
we observed a dome flying to heaven
and with a spy-glass we saw in it
two beautiful ladies singing.

6. Most of the public affairs are decided at night.
The revenue to government is 60,000,000
but when government goes to war
the people gave the wonderful sum of 840 millions
the whole of which is spent.

7. If a man gets short of millions of money
he would be obliged to leave the celebrated London.

8. One of the twelve viziers of government
is called the High Lord of the Admiralty.
Their ships are like forests.
They have always been victorious over their enemies.

9. The water of the river Thames is very heavy
and not at all good for the digestion
nor could it ever produce an appetite.
Yet the people of this country do not use water as a drink
when it is necessary they take a little
once in three or four days
even the viziers do not drink water
without the advice of each other.

10. In every street
there is the light
of many thousand moons
put together.

11. Before this time
within a period of two hundred and ninety years
the people were wild beings
that lived under the shadow of the trees.
They dressed in the skins of animals
and if they had a king they sometimes killed him
and likewise the kings killed many of the people.
Many were obliged to go to the New World.

12. They conduct their affairs with perfect prudence
so that they have no governors
they obey their laws
even their houses are numbered
their love of liberty is measureless.

13. Not a single person begs in the streets
there may be 7,000,000 poor
but if there should be any one begging
he would be taken up immediately and punished.

14. They say writing is good enough if it can be read.

15. Their object is to keep the world in tranquillity
their policy is that war would take away
the security and happiness of the people
and their commerce much injured.
For this important principle they have a Board of Trade
and Offices of Insurance with millions of capital.

16. They seek very much after news
every person is acquainted with the Government
many times a learned private individual becomes a prime minister.
It is the duty of the House of Commons
to take care that not a halfpenny is spent in vain.

17. The treasury has a vizier to present the accounts
that every soul may know how the money was spent

and in case he should see any thing wrong
has a right to rise up in the House of Commons
and seize the vizier by the collar
saying
What have you done with my money?

18. The tories in ancient days have always been in office
and thereby they have established to themselves some privileges
by which every tory is now a possessor of millions of money.

19. What they call newspapers are written by some clever
editors and poets. They enjoy the confidence of the people.

20. Every person that may want to send a letter
has only to address it regularly
and send it to the boxes in every direction about the town.
All the letters are brought to the large department of the Post-office
where the lord vizier resides.
Afterwards they put each mail in a separate bag.

21. A few miles distance from every town
there are placed some pots or kettles of iron.
They put every day in them thousands of tons
of the mineral coals which they burn
until the coals become dissolved like a black liquid.
To every pot there is a pipe
through which all the gas runs into a cistern.
On the top of this there is a tower
in the shape of a trumpet.
To this there is a very large pipe
joined to several other pipes
through which the gas is conducted to
myriads of houses of fifty or a hundred rooms
each to receive this light from one pipe
to the head of which there is an instrument
in the shape of a lion.

22. All their shops are magnificently built of marble
beautifully adorned with large glass windows.
In none of their houses do you see any fly or moskito.

23. The marriages in this country are conducted as follows:
young men must first receive complete education in mathematics
and other branches of useful learning.
The young females also receive a suitable education.
They do not usually marry under twenty years of age.
Their connexion commences as follows:
the young bachelors go out to parks and gardens
to smell the fresh air.

24. They have ascertained that besides the known seven planets
there are four others and that the earth turns on its axis
like the others and that each of the planets is
thickly inhabited by beings like those of this world.

25. From the house of the ambassador of Rome
any one can have an excellent view of those angelic forms
who take their walk or ride in the Park.

26. Twelve miles out of London
on the river Thames
there is a very large city
wholly devoted to the purpose of war.
Praise be to God!
What immense power
has he given to these people.

27. 'It is four months since I came to this country'
Mohammed Ismael Khan's harem complained
'where I have not seen any one of the believers.'

Letter to Timothy Donnelly
dated 2 a.m. 26 Dec 2011

'As a child I found it difficult to sleep.
I couldn't put an end to the saying of things.'

Dear Timothy me too and it only gets worse
as I get older but here's something I read

in Mayhew's account of a London
snake-swallower. The head of the snake

with 'the stingers cut out' goes 'about an inch
and a half down the throat and the rest of it

continues in the mouth, curled round.' So where
do the swallower's words go in the meantime?

You and I now we aren't children would write
them down but probably the swallower could

no more have done this than you or I when
we were two or three and in any case I've found

it doesn't help very much. As for the snakes
'they're smooth one way' – he meant when they're

going down – but the scales like things said
'rough you a bit when you draw them up.'

Amongst

           other matters
in the *Daily Mirror*
4 Sept 1939 –

the instructions to treat
scaremongers like a case of smallpox
and take your gold coins
to sell to the Treasury –

the assurances that monuments
to human achievement
will be preserved
and the day will come
when our traditional
liberties will be restored –

the explanations of
what hand rattles mean
and what to do
if your feet puff and swell –
blame stale Foot Acid –

but thank God
for the Ruler of the King's Navee
not forgetting Popeye & Porky Goldburg
& the 1000 short-term prisoners
unconditionally released –

amongst the requests
not to crowd together
not to let your radio blare
not to carry your gas-mask
like Lady Hoare –

& leaving aside
Wag Write Mrs Toodles Love Josie –

amongst all this –

'Today's ruling number is Six
and its colour vibration Light Blue.'

Mutability Cento:
a Sheffield cacophony for 10 or more voices

& for Adam Piette & Ágnes Lehóczky

still no idea where it was exactly
round the corner from Tudor Square
the paste land later than Ruskin's time
from when it was the Naughty Girls' Home
That our daughters may be as corner stones
the picture wouldn't help you to recognise
only 2 months later
the best view is if you go up somebody's steps
a little way from Bell Hagg Road
it was a tragedy they shoe-horned
it into a Millennium box
 how many and where
 the public toilets used to be
 I can recall Fitzalan Square
 glazed roof and fancy tiling
 Surrey Street with goldfish in the cisterns
 Moorhead (not sure)
a long shaft revolved close to the ceiling
on the third or fourth floor which diverted
the power by a drive belt to the buffing machines
I think it was called Cadman Lane
it shows the Electric Light Works on the map but that
was the factory opposite I was mixing it up with
there was a quadrangle and Housing used the front part
they called the Manager the ghost because
he glided in and out and he mumbled
so posh that no-one understood
 and next to the library at Highfields
 some on the corner of London Road & Queens Road
 at the junction of Cemetery Road & Sharrow Lane
 one Top of Toyne Street Crookes
Where did Pearl Street go

before someone put ashes down
Pearl Street was great sledging
one of the girls that lived near the gennel
tried to get us talking Dog Latin
I went round to sweaty Betty's
on the corner of Priory Road
 one on Bramall Lane
 one for men only just up the road from the Wicker
 the one opposite the Hallamshire
 a nice little cottage turned into a cafe
 also a sarnie shop at Crosspool
 by the Cemetery entrance
a staircase took you up on the roof overlooking the river
at tempered springs at warren street on heavy springs
the building's still there but the company's gone
zoom in on the sign and you'll get the picture
the writing's bad hard to read
what's left of it's a body parlour right on effingham street
ted phoenix was a fitter there and tinny joe hell
and the Little Sisters of the Poor
allowed in on the shop floor
 gents next to the Broadfield
 up for rent as a kiosk
 and next to the White lion
 part of the train station
 sat atop that wall
no it's not the right place
the right place is 50 or 60 yards further down
and about 30 feet upwards where the brick walls are
but that isn't where Mulligan's Mansions was
someone told me the doorway on the other side
was the entrance to Heeley Station
a long dark tunnel with three offshot ramps
most likely where an old City used to be
the mortar's only one layer thick
something to do with the drain pipes
as there's two enormous valves

    ladies and gent at Hillsbrough
    now part of Mr Tse's restuant
    or something like that
    and what about the ones
    perched over the Sheaf
    where it joins the Don
the santas grotto with a row of fountains
lit up at the bottom of the moor
when it went from london road to leopold street
an old bomb site before the Manpower building
market stalls there on market days
you had to go through a kind of maze made of picket fencing
to where the lorry parked up for the Polio injections
huge queue waiting to be stabbed by the man with the blunt needle
    one on Commonside
    another on Heavygate Road
    structures still there but bricked up
    also underground ones down Dixon Road
    near the Rag & Tag
a small shooting gallery with two 35mm cinema projectors
on the left as you went in
I'd cut up a side street from Abbeydale Road
a steep shortcut from the rickety bridge across from Heeley Baths
near a Temperance Bar that sold good Sarsaparilla
a proper snug
wood panels and pumps
that was Tony di Donno's
    Blonk Street bridge bricked up
    Bridge Street bus station
    the Hole in the Road
    as always full as it was smelly
that's sure to bring up Pond Street Nora
I heard she ran off with the Duke of Darnall
who directed traffic in his frock coat and spats
he wasn't deaf and dumb when Big Albert moved him on
Nora had a child in the change and it was taken off her
she ate all the heads off the tulips

the policeman I don't think it was Albert
it could have been Popeye
said he wouldn't piss on her if she was on fire
 Mushroom Lane at the side of Weston Park
 some at sheffield lane top now a cafe
 the little gem at Nethergreen
 with the burnt orange curved glazed bricks
 one in Archer Road
 someone said she'd love to rebuild
 as a garden folly
the buses revved their engines from about ten past eleven
nothing worse than a non-starter at that time of night
then the insects
inspectors blew their whistles
Acme Thunderers five minutes later
we were always in the tingalary track
Commercial Street to you
Comical to me
they liked to be first off the grid
and beat the lights before the whistle
 The loggia-style one on Ecclesall Rd South
 one on wellington street
 and garden street near the old drinking fountain
where's the You Are Here map gone
when you pressed the buttons little bulbs lit up
showing where places were
a contortionist could lean on them all
there were always some that didn't work
 one made of green slate (gents)
 in the middle of Meadow Street
 the Ringinglow ones
 now a Rocking Horse Shop
the whale was in a glass fronted case
long dangly things in its mouth
it was dead and they were moving
it round on the back of an artic
it was someone near Ponsfords

I meant somewhere
>   on the left at the traffic lights on Rutland Road
>   the remains of a Gents only

Wrong road never wrong
>   High Green had one at the corner of the park

Nothing by Nobody:
An Interrupted Reading of
Burton's *Anatomy*, 2011

Feb 1

neminis nihil
           imaginis imago
reading looking backwards
through the philter of cognitive theory
Hymenoptera Hypersensitivity
in an Imported Fire Ant Endemic Area
(sent to Anticyra they arrive by analogy
allergy or chance in Academe)

if as I have read
they were afternoon-men born of mushrooms
The Lord shall smite them with the botch of Egypt
(in a swarm of bees
President Obama backs President Mubarak)

Feb 2

fake hackers claiming
vigil coma & many hard words
philosophers explode
larvae, lawyers, lemures
tumults, combustions, uproars, Abaddon
ut in Ægypto
           per iram et odium
The president's plain-clothes devils let loose
a hyperpathic variety of February's malady
wolf-madness

Feb 4

disorder of time and place
sudden death and what not
frothy spectrums and the like

for 'bangle' read 'bungle'
Balance it O Lord You have an incoming payment
(Mubarak turns his back on Obama
for not backing him enough,
if he did)
contra gentes
           contra Manichæos
'their president Mercury had no better fortune'
inertia entertainment shared by noble gases
but whatever the younger Pliny said
Trajan
for all his wars
survives in no epos
but one stonker of a column
with St Peter on top

Feb 5

in the shop of humours:
fountains & furtherers
overmuch cockering
cases of conscience in
a case of leather
every word in its misconster
shoeing-horns of idleness
incondite voices
Middle East policies
spintriae aplenty
obsolete gestures
new coats for the moon

Feb 6

eyes in his throat and a library
printed in the roof of his mouth
Dear Sir I have 70kg of gold dust
I do not know much about

'in his Anatomy of Melancholy Francis Bacon'
aka William Sheikh-Peer, The Ancient Sage
aka Elias Artifex, Theophrastian master of the Rosie Cross
aka Kidhr, The Green One, patron of the Sufi orders

differing as an egg and a chestnut
a rash of stars like so many nails in a door

'those two green children that fell from heaven'
or clambered up from St Martin's Land
but I'd sooner believe William of Newburgh
than anything said
by our man in Cairo Mister Blair

Feb 7

when time was entertained by footnotes

[1] Erycius Poteanus
in his *Pietatis Thaumata* (Antwerp: 1617)
published 1022 permutations in classical hexameter
of Bernard Bauhuis' monostich
Tot tibi sunt dotes, Virgo, quot sidera cælo.
Why stop? We mustn't suppose Poteanus
ran out of ideas and despaired.
There were 1022 visible stars in Ptolemy's heaven
and the Virgin could have no more virtues than that.

[2] To whom does Rainnerus of Lüneburg
owe his immortality? *Pace* Burton

the *Proteus Poeticus* was the work of Gregor Kleppis
welcoming three noblemen to Dresden
in 1617. It contains 1617 permutations of
Dant tria jam Dresdæ, ceu sol dat, lumina lucem.
To whom the nobles owe
whatever remains of their sunlight
is an ordinary question. Rainnerus
has meanwhile been deprived of
$2150 - 1617 = 533$ permutations.

Feb 8

Dear Sir
Re yours of 6th inst.
I have digged out of that broody hill
a chaos of receipts
nonsense-confused compounds
indefensible much magnified enchantments
a gown of giants' beards for austere times
tinfoiled happiness (I quote, it was translated from the Latin)
as many tempests in tosspots as fatal engines
gripings expressed in most careful verse
& last but not least
several nonentities of potable gold

Do not be transposed
Dear Sir
Let experience determine

All Told

for Judith Goldman

Was it my anxiety's naivety
or was it
the other way round from the start?

We don't want any neuro-mantics here
in a state of vivid sensation

We don't want any of
that poetry or wistful thinking or people
who wear their hats inside their heads

You see self-assurance
but let me reassemble
self-erasure

for it's a necessary labor
to set the writing certain
that the reading may be sure

Richard Mulcaster said that?

Yes he did and now all
the world's someone else's chatroom

& because
I woke up this morning
& unzipped an Arabic zephyr
& saw that 0
was nothing but a balmy breeze
or an ode to Revolution
I at last understand that strange
word 'number'

O fatal tables
or as the Vodafone ad says
(cosmic pies she miscopies)
'Use the code you must'
(microscopic she miscopies)
which I'd put down to
(whatshername, Miss Epic)
crystallised losses
(O no)
or a funeral achievement
(this name has already been taken)

(please choose another)

Les Hiboux, or the 19th Century & After

Either it's strange that
waking-up gloom's best
read after midnight
or it's the art of rhyme.
When exactly 'to see
the object as it really is not'
although that's Wilde on
the critic's not the poet's
aim's still a question in the
malflorist's debt. When for
example are owls not owls?
When they're calling *ennui
ennui*? And what's a morning-
after without souvenirs?

Austerity Sonnet

―― ‐ ―― deviance
―― ‐ ‐ ―― monitory
―― ―― ‐ defiance
―――― ‐ ‐ monetary

―― ‐ ―― ‐ revenants
―― ―― ‐ ―― herald
‐ ‐ ―― ‐ ―― resonance
‐ ―― ―― ―― heard

―― ―― ―― oriental
―― ‐ ‐ ―― ‐ unique
‐ ―― ―― rational
‐ ―― ―― unquiet

―― ―― ‐ ―― menaces
―― ‐ ―― ―― nemesis

In Their Manner of Speaking: Directions Towards a Performance in Mime of *Our Mutual Friend*

for Peter Robinson

[*The characters are all present on a dark stage. They perform only when spotlit, sometimes solo, sometimes in duets or trios, in various permutations which possibly replot the novel.*]

Eugene Wrayburn leaning back with a heavy sigh, drowsily
Lizzie Hexam mournfully opening her eyes to look on the ground
Bella Wilfer eyelids drooping, coldly tossing her curls
Mrs Wilfer adjusts the handkerchief under her chin, resignedly
John Rokesmith/Harmon with a glance and a half-smile, gently
Wrayburn arms folded, disparaging, eyes shut, enjoying his cigar
Silas Wegg musing, nodding with an air of gentle resignation
Noddy Boffin smiling, left arm nursing his knotted stick
Wegg bestirring himself to take precaution, feelingly, sulkily
Boffin leans forward with confidential dignity, alarmed appeal
Mrs Boffin smoothing her dress with an air of immense enjoyment
John with an air of reluctance, deference, earnestness, hesitating
Bella with a little stamp of her foot, pointing her forefinger merrily
Mrs W with a dignified bend of her head, with an indignant shiver
Wegg one arm a-kimbo, with modesty, with increasing complacency
Boffin one hand to his chin, crumpling a blotted note in the other
Mrs B clapping hands, gaily rocking to and fro, laying aside her shawl
John with a quick turn, correcting himself, perfectly composed, soothing
Wrayburn with the air of a philosopher lecturing a disciple, vexedly
Rogue Riderhood fumbling with an old sodden fur cap, with a leer
Lizzie in some confusion, as a recollection flashes upon her
Wegg as if beginning to regard himself in quite a new light
Boffin takes a piece of chalk from his pocket, abstractedly
Wrayburn plaintive, with gravity, perplexed, inquisitive
Riderhood shading his mouth with his hand, ducking, with a servile air
Bradley Headstone with pale and quivering lips, eyes averted
Lizzie with hands now covering her anxious face, with starting tears
Jenny Wren screws up her eyes and chin, looks prodigiously knowing

Bella as if italicising with a twist of dimpled chin, energetically
Boffin wiping his mouth with an air of much refreshment
John forming the syllables of the word 'nonsense' on his lips
Headstone wiping the starting perspiration from his face, despairingly
Jenny with an angry little shake of her right fist close before her eyes
Headstone shakes from head to foot, with a clutch at the breast of his shirt
Bella looks comically frightened, with childish gravity
Rumty Wilfer with his hand to his eyes, dubiously, mildly
Jenny looking through her screwed-up fist like an opera glass
Headstone protesting with errant hands, in a half-suffocated way
Jenny holds out her hand, looking upward, her needle pricking the air
Wegg nodding with an air of friendly recognition, condoling
Boffin with a glance of discomfiture, rubbing his ear
Mrs B with left hand thoughtfully touching her brow, placidly
Bella lays the forefinger of her glove on her lip
John patient but proud, looking steadily, with beaming face
Mrs W apostrophises the air with scornful fortitude, sublime severity
Rumty apologetic, his hand enjoining patience, with trepidation
Wegg cheering up bravely, slowly, knowingly, exasperated
Riderhood beats his open right hand on the palm of his left
Headstone folding his hands before him, unfolding them
Lizzie with indignation she cannot repress, raising her eyes
Wrayburn with determination, calmest indifference, contrition
Wegg nodding with an air of insinuating frankness
Boffin staring at the moon, with commiseration, a little staggered
Bella with eyes looking away, slaps herself with her glove
John excitedly, joyfully, fondly, coaxingly, laughing outright
Rumty meditating, stoutly, cherubically, approvingly
Mrs W assuming a deadly cheerfulness, an awful air of politeness
Mrs B draws a long breath, laughs with childlike glee
Headstone with a lumbering show of ease, stolid, vacant, self-communing
Riderhood knuckling his forehead, backing a little, snapping his fingers
Lizzie with an incredulous smile, with a look of supplication
Wrayburn again folding his arms, candidly, as if he were a little stung
Headstone trying to constrain his working mouth, with a stab at the sky
Riderhood smiting his right leg, head aslant, stubbornly chewing

Wrayburn with a look of appeal, indecision, rallying
Lizzie trembling, resolute
John keeping his countenance, interrogatively
Bella turning suddenly, putting out her right foot, with a loving laugh
Boffin wrinkling his face into a map of curves and corners
Rumty with a flagrant assumption of unconsciousness

[*Our Mutual Friend* concerns itself in various ways with literacy and legibility. 'All print is shut to me,' laments Boffin; he and several other characters would have no access to the speeches Dickens attributes to them – their spoken words have in effect been taken away and hidden from them. Suppose, then, that speech were removed from the novel and we were granted only Dickens' accounts of his characters' *manners* of speaking – then we have mime and we have stepped into that popular drama Dickens so loved. Mime is nevertheless a conscious demonstration that the gulf between gesture and its description, whether or not shut in print, belongs to a different order of legibility, briefly touched upon in Wrayburn's remarks on 'that very word, Reading, in its critical use'. The extent to which the characters in *Our Mutual Friend* are illegible to each other is in part due to their levels of literacy – and yet, in great part, not.]

Frugal Fractals

Jetzeit has been looked up 188 times
favorited 0 times
listed 0 times
commented on 0 times
and is not a valid Scrabble word.

We don't have any examples for jetzeit
but we're constantly adding material
so please check back soon.

*

Mrs Comfort Baker
from her hospital bed
offers me I hesitate
to say a lifetime's dough
if I'll be the house
of the Lord's caretaker.

Mrs Comfort Baker
the Lord forbids.
I know it's only
short-lived brass but
I'll drop your name
in a verse instead.

*

So many years on earth
spent putting into words
the essence and precise
relations of the Trinity

but arrived by ship
they tripped off the tongue
or gangplank if you must.
'Slavery, disease & Christianity.'

*

that bottle-blonde MP
last night on the talk show
'proud to be a daughter of Thatcher'
(too young to remember)
if it had been a murder mystery
it wouldn't have been much of a mystery
she did it

*

Off Nominal

either the wake of
as compared to the normal
breakout manoeuvres

Whereas requirements
typically specify
normal system behaviour

they are often
woefully
incomplete

*

after the Chinese

November night snow.
A fox pads down Crescent Road.
In Brisbane England reach
500-1 in their 2nd innings.
But even though *Jetzeit*
has been checked 56 times
in the last 3 months it's the same
old story: 'no image found'.

*

A Note on Dichotomy

'Organise.' Archival
archrivals won't recognise
what the other one means.
Meanwhile 'cascade'

a lovely word digital-
isation did for
is daily resurrected
in newsreader italic.

*

'in a quite otherguess light'
when blot becomes plot or vice versa
the sudden revelation of
'homemade skin on morris piper chips'
(patatine fritte fatte in casa)
or fossilised caterpillar footprints
philosophised in capitalist firepits

*

Most of the estimates were inmates
of the house of funny numbers.
Dear Frances none of them could count.
If you asked them 'What's 60?'
they'd fiddle with their fingers & thumbs
then sooner or later
they'd hit on the answer
it's a row of standing stones
curling back on itself at one end
and placed next to
more graceful & accurate than
a circle
an ellipse.

*

Ave atque vale
mon semblable mon frère

Catullus might have said that
but not Byron. Byron didn't

like to welcome very much
but he'd probably have settled

for hypocrite lecteur
& never missed an opportunity

to bid anyone Farewell.

In an Annex of the Gallery at the End of Time

a video plays on a loop. It shows footage of Tony Blair addressing his army in the desert. He is as usual over-excited in the company of uniformed men, his eyes moist and shiny but face slightly coy. His shirt sleeves flutter not with desert wind but sexual tension which is released along his arms, through the stiffened elbows. The straightened fingers of both hands jab together as if to punctuate his speech but they beat their own rhythm. Then his palms open to the sky, double-jointed thumbs pointing earthward – the caption beneath the monitor quotes a couplet from Juvenal's Third Satire in Dryden's translation, revised by a graffiti artist:

        un   People's express
Where /influenc'd by the ~~Rabble's bloody~~ will,
               he un   s
With Thumbs bent back, ~~they~~ /popularly kill/.

*

When we visit the gallery again the video has changed. This is later footage: Blair's eyes now dark in their sockets, skin wrinkled but tight beneath the cheekbones, hair receded. Death's Head in a book of emblems, or Poussin Parodied: The Dance To The Music Of Time on fast forward, in Arcadia an Echo: he is delivering the speech which announces The Triumph Over Global Warming. The words EUROPEAN COMMUNITY are blazoned behind him but as the camera zooms in the outer letters disappear and the death's head seems an oversize dot concealing the first N. Perhaps he is the necromancer who turned up on peak-time TV instead of David Blaine; but PEA.COM, we make of this what we will.

*

Torched in the riots of August 2011 the gallery was closed for a year. The final video shows the reopening ceremony. Pan across the Olympic legacy touts. Johnson. Coe. The ghosts of Jowell and Red Ken's pigeons. Miliband mimicking Blair's gestures but Blair himself or perhaps the body double he used in his heyday is the keynote speaker. He is announcing his second coming but we only know this by watching the movement of his hands and shoulders. The mic wasn't working and lipreading doesn't help. His mouth is drawn more tightly on his mask than on the regularest guy that ever graced Bonfire Night.

Austerity Stuffing

they may have been
the aerodynamic model
for stealth bombers
but what buzz & clatter
shieldbugs make
on target practice
at midnight

or

The first person who looked up
Tetra methyl diamino benzehydryl phosphinous
found it hadn't yet been tagged.

'My aim of writing is not to know you
as I have no interest of knowing you
and would not like to know you
unless if needs be.'

or

That once in concealment –
that nip in omnipresence –
farewell free will – why it
took so long you'll find
end up in a preface –
but while the dictionary's
open – you're safe –

or

Dark arts desecrated Descartes!
Socrates secretes dead certs!
Fortress vortices cavort!
Thoughtless votaries default!

(Don't tell latterday economists.
They're all working men. When they're
not frontloading they're backfilling.)

or

Apuleius glossed
in the passage
of a godless page –

You – I –

romantic-aromatic
caught-out castaway
in Melville's wake

or

acorns & atoms &
Tom's a-torn

they sing & it
does so happen that

worlds & trees &
trickster-fixers

collide & collude

or

Heritage heartache –
folded gold of
Neothomist nomads –

NEMO ROOD DOOR OMEN

– what pensive-perverse
power-powder of a new-year
nightmare's this?

or

one Manichaean candidate's lament
repaid in the latent
thee's & thou's of a baffled
tho' rapid ballad

(opinion's opponent
abased – abated – beckoned
or not – betokened – or so-so)

or

as if money were subject
to the laws of physics while
allowing for bankers' remorse

some carrion creation
of molecule-molehills

vagueness at the edges
vengeance at the core

or

what to do with bendy
notions of Being or
modes of survival in this
deignage as we say –

there you have me –

stunned by numbers
plain as a pin

or

logogriffins stand guard
against boredom-prospectors
writing reading reading writing

Messrs I & I
hybridised as house-plants

such books could be written
if anyone had patience

or

themeless anthem
rolling news on the Lockjaw channel
when absence wants alibis
harsher than hush ever was

or so Obvious the Pilgrim
labile as a lullaby
told Oblivious his brother

or

Such a no-man-clatter –
a newfound Gehenna to tame time in –
the deipnosophists
are setting things aright.

What goes for the above
will apply with slight variants below.

One more symposium should do it.

or

'so long as there's
pizza & soccer-circenses' –

BESPOKE SPECIES ALERT
SHAM CHAOS BECALMED –

you there shush –

you – cynic crystal –

shush shush

Cachemphaton

Northland Macaronic

Bæ bæ lille lam
har du någon ull?

Ja baas ja baas
jeg har kroppen full

Søndagsklær til far
söndagskjol åt mor

Och två par strumpor
åt lillebror
dat bibbert van de kou

[Baa baa li'l lamb
have you any wool?

Yes boss yes boss
a body crop full

Sunday trousers for pa
a sunday skirt for ma

And two pairs o' socks
for li'l bro
who shivers in the col']

From the Horse's Mouth:
A Transcript & Homage to Dr Swift

Ideal weither fivoiired the Victoria
Auteur Ittrf Club vcsteidiv for ills an
jiual living Dab litanies the attendance
at time meeting n tile is flecked by the
absence fiom town of many iiultir ac
mg people but licit it pelted to be a good
gathering western I to o first favourites
won hut tile victim o two out tillers quite
evened Ion stoic Ice ii in vv is inter
casino eva ii eases of direful merger
once cain helenc the stir endive those rids
who decided to suspend Hie well I known
jockey I Killoin nr viv month, and V

Murrell who lode the Steeplechase win
lier foil one mouth Ihev also lined It
Williet lid mad cautioned P lent lily
isarctssi piovielcd t coition in Hie Hope
ton up When le tiling tile held be
three lengths he run off it the fall turn
Vib t pipit nile I that lit she bolted
twist loud tile coin e mil tilt I tried to
lum the outside I ills new u tile point echoic
she lug nigiiiilv um nil llei little
riddle lid 1 due illi vi as tin own on and he
sustained a bl till en t illat lone

nicit eoinmcnttd with the Moby I
Hurdle Poe loin which Hine weie nine
runnel Hobgoblin vi is its favour
item Hough lie oak I if mi lum it exalt
on the big side Quite I mint it lid id I
tiling at pi t mill in H in it is led foil is

furloiifi! mad then llolroblin took the
leal Tight lineal lump I e m over the hill
unit vi t in ii not alone, the t tile iv midi
lurk Remitis who I iel chopped hie!
lit pulle I nap loving 1 icily can lion In
terribly h 1 moil Hit sti light tend over t

last hurdle winch he bungle cl ft um Spoils
up and O! I Hu list nine 1 finished
t ti null and lent longoicnin be half I
legit lid tuts I in I t fun Hind anti
lelhcr fern the with livid list ii! tin vv to
Hie mini w is well but eel it (I lo 1

Le Testament de Mr Pepys

there never having been
any music here
better than ballads

I

pour rancontrer la femme de je sais quoy
    à faire ce que je voudrais
jo haze todo which I had a corasón
    but I did natha sino besar her

ce que je voudrais avec la mosa
    uno ombre pouvait avoir done any cosa
con laquelle je faisais almost whatever
    but I did natha sino besar her

hazer what I tena a mind para faire
    tocando sa cosa con mi cosa
que je sum demasiado kind jo creo
    but I did natha sino besar her

II

la fille hath something assez jolie
did suffer me a la besar mucho
I did con mi mano tocar sa jambe
               à mon content

jo did give ella 20 solidos
in time may come para laisser me hazer
con su mano tocando mi cosa
               à mon content

I did hazer whatever I would
con mi mano sino tocar la chose même
and hazendo la cosa par cette moyen
                à mon content

III

yo quisere hasta a hazer me hazer
the moher erat expecting mi venida
yo haze what yo vellum cum her
sed by and by su marido came in

yo should poner mi mano abaxo ses jupes
and lie comme jo voudrais upon lo lectum
todo la cosa con much voluptas
sed by and by su marido came in

mauvais amours which yo be merry for
I did besarlas muchas et tocar
I aime her de todo mi corazon
sed by and by su marido came in

IV

the otra day quand yo was con her
    parlar the esta that yo did
creo I might have hecho algo
                con grand plaisir

ella weeping still I did beso la
    voudrais haver hazer algo with her
todo la otra cosa con ella
                con grand plaisir

my mind did run après her todo the night
    ponendo her mano upon mi cosa
aussi besar her belle ancilla
                  con grand plaisir

H.C. Earwicker's Train Ride

*for Alec & the trains
which didn't leave the station*

CUTPURSE ROW

    (The past has never been so close that sirens sang.
    Clog and gutter gold beyond her door
    in the windows fades.)

JOHN A'DREAMS MEWS

    (Thor's hammer on a slate-grey hackle
    like a great ship broken in a mudcat yard.
    Hump reckons roadkill.)

FLAGGY BRIDGE

    (Add a placamerk:
    thixotropic slurry, level now falling.
    Eclogites of psammites.)

HATCHETTSBURY ROAD

    (Divide and conquer moaning
    as though it were sheets
    leaving a mint and a complimentary bottle.)

NUNSBELLY SQUARE

    (His for with he you
    I that as on
    it is all was.)

GLINTYLOOK

    (Boys boys!
    Evangelion chased away
    ole Boogeyman.)

TURNAGAIN LANE

    (Latlong data of an old gaol deal.
    Has any one herd what is become of it?
    To avoid confusion they cannot goe through.)

Change here for

OLD VICO ROUNDPOINT

    (50 Halo's of transparent Fronch sperm
    Ex Woodlark from Souraboya damnaed by soa water
    for Unreserved bale. Torms, cash.)

RIVAPOOL

    (Where the tradition existed fought
    either it was made an even
    or it tangled once to the gooseflesh.)

WHATALOSE

    (Inis actualld Poseidonn countreio
    not make you thinkzhou Bandice of coloive.
    O look for all fourt, see Jim.)

INCUBONE

    (Dragonair of Italy?
    Inest Coeli Aureliani?
    Shutter Island? Platinum candy?)

TWO-TONGUE COMMON

    (Forked or cloven
    glossa or dialektos
    they go like mill clap.)

BOTHERSBY NORTH

    (How Either mat purity and Or glory Be
    Bluetooth'd it – Gretzky'd it –
    Got going with a Greek defence.)

KHUMMER-PHET

    (Some who foresee say
    tertia par urbis probably
    small and flat in remembrance.)

The Clinamen Transfigured

for Steve McCaffery

'a tradition attentive to linguistic microparticles, [...] the telluric affiliations of language which achieve an ontological contour in the Lucretian theory of the *clinamen*, the world-inaugurating swerve of atoms (and/as the word-inaugurating activity of letters)'

Imagining Language in Istanbul

'to put it another way, "world" is what emanates from the line or cut, the bifurcation of the blank into opposing components (symmetrical or asymmetrical)'

From the Portico of Santa Maria in Trastevere

'Conceived as atoms, letters are events strictly defined by their dynamics, and being perpetually volatile they introduce deviance as the basic rule of all *grammata*.'

Boston Test-Pit: A Mystery

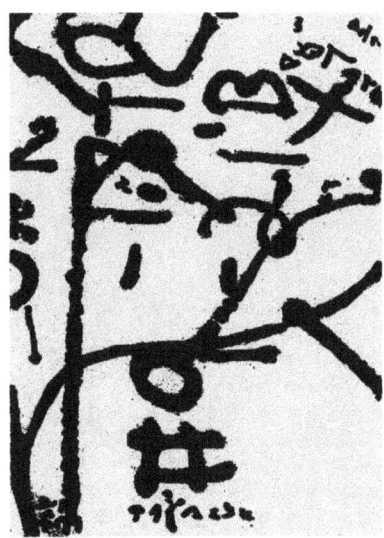

'As the being-of-movement, the clinamen becomes apparent to itself only in the disappearance of stabilities. Like a slip of the tongue, the clinamen is less a performance than a happening.'

Elegy Written in a Lancashire Churchyard

'[Giordano] Bruno effectively reduces the minimal vector of the clinamen from a swerve in primary articulation (i.e., a deviation and difference among letters) to a gestural declination of the prelettristic mark.'

Penmon Priory Revisited

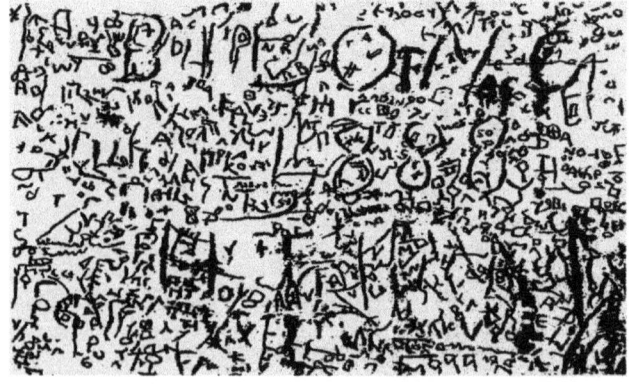

'The spaciousness evoked here is a reminder that, in Epicurean cosmology, the contextual prerequisite of atoms is a void. We might say by analogy that void is to atoms what space and *différance* are to letters.'

Another Attempt at Imagining Language in Istanbul

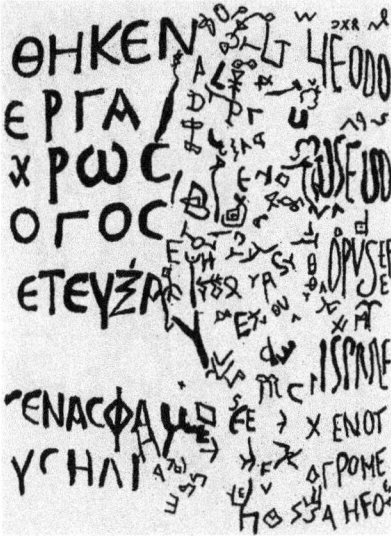

'The Lucretian legacy begets a sense of the letter as both "precise" and "inexact"; the atom-letter is libido without organ, both slave and master, compliant component and maverick principle in one.'

Return to the Portico

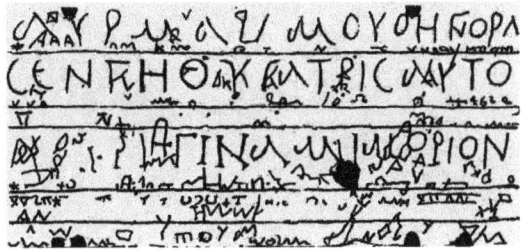

'the clinamen, the initiatory swerve into intelligible semiosis. The proper way to describe the clinamen is *gratuitous*'

Hardwick Hallmarks

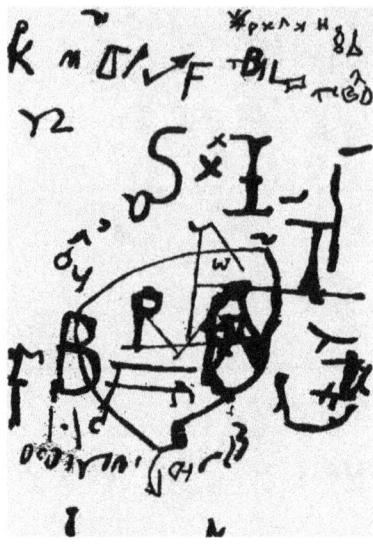

'as a law governing the exception rather than the rule, the Lucretian swerve is a 'pataphysical phenomenon par excellence'

On a Bishop laid to rest in Wells Cathedral

'A disturbing but informing particularity, the clinamen is swerve as *inclination*, initiating the body's erotic profundity.'

Istanbul in *Jetzeit*

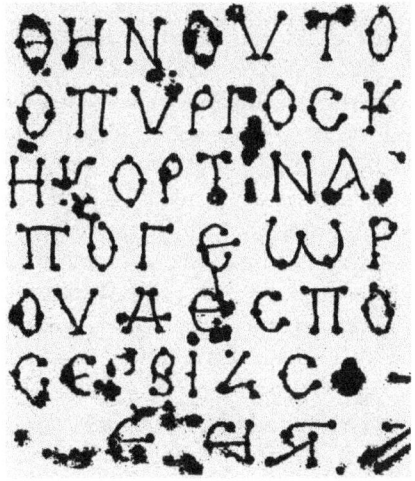

'their concertina cities still unfolding
local news reports of regional clinamens'

Imagining Language on the Beach at Kilve

'There is never something "lost" in translation without something
else being *found*. We are impaired only by our dream of identity, the
futile wish for all languages to attain a central equivalence, a balanced
correspondence.'

[All but one of the quotations are from Jed Rasula & Steve McCaffery *Imagining Language* (MIT Press, 1998), mostly from the essay on the clinamen, pages 532-538. The caption to 'Istanbul in *Jetzeit*' is from McCaffery's poem 'Novel 85'.

The graphics are extracted from an open-ended work, *Transcriptions Pending Translation*. They share their photographic base (sometimes an identical image) with the visuals appearing in my collaboration with Steve McCaffery, *Paradigm of the Tinctures* (Granary Books, 2007, reissued in a revised and expanded edition as an Argotist ebook, 2010) but the swerve here is in precisely the opposite direction: there the treatment was painterly, looking for depth of colour and offering Steve possibilities of ekphrasis which he by turns swerved towards and away from; here the clinamen returns the language-objects photographed to the inscriptional gesture made by successive human hands in co-operation or perhaps more alluringly con-fusion with their material medium (usually stone) and the weather – 'the elements'.]

Cachemphaton

'Quintilian gives the example
of using the nominative
form of *intercapedinis*,
intercapedo ("interruption"),
since its last two syllables
could sound like
pedo, "I break wind".'

Funnily enough
the third syllable of
cachemphaton itself presents
an English speaker
with a similar problem

and in any case, Smart-arse,
so to speak,
check the Related Figure
Cacozelia

which you probably
thought was a female
character's name in a
play by Alfred Jarry

but not so. It is
'The use of
foreign words
to make the speaker
appear learned.'

An Internet Sieve for Aretino's Positions

1. There fotterem Eve and Adam
trovarno die so that the dishonest
mangiavan not that fruit traitor
I know that sfoiavano lovers
all pleasures of the fortunate witness

2. Dear old man
to put a good game
leads to no reputation
the best bits
eat the grease pan below the fire
in this other culture
which is really a bird
and cracks in a building

3. This gem is worth more than gold ch'un
to observe decorum
Mistress mine
anyone who deserves a Cristero cold water
ruthless and proud
we'll keep after him

4. Hard or soft on the bed with cultural dances
I am a forfante and a villain
known as a horse a horse
and if you don't want it go get with God

5. I prov'or so solemn
Indulge yourself

6. Because I keep my hands where his feet are
You're a beast and you will not be done
I want you to many cul Mamin
And I know well who is the sweetest ch'il scratch
I have a job any valent'uomo in this

7. Say grace behind or in front?
I go a Friar Mariano, verbs gratia
And take him with his hand
I'll die if we fottiam among us

8. And while a coglioneria sary
I'm not doing the cul famine
Finish me in my genealogy
the round is different from the idiot
that the aquatic Malvasia
let me in between the old scorched
ch'anch'io if man he was

9. As if I vo 'test? as if I can?
But if I v'infrango
thrown into a bed and also in the brush above me
that if it were Marforio or a giant
I n'averò solace

10. I want in the culture
because this is a food prelate
plunge here as the one in command
I accept, my dear
spingel by hand
but we want to stay a year behind

11. While I yearn for you he is me
fed to the whim of improviso
I n'incaco you Franciosa
that this pleasure arciperfetto
intrarei in a well without a bucket

12. I am not Mars I am Hercules Rangone
and if you were here my rebec
my sweet wife
I fear that love does not give me
hill machinations

13. One day I promise you
you net it out
or will I now and when you
give me all the linguine
alas
O God

14. Do not pull the wheelbarrow
and if you
Beatrice
is slow I forgive you because
if not for that I would just

15. Among the thousands you've had
ch'un villan web surfing cottage cheese
how I'd enjoy an abbess

16. Because we had done and sleep
I am happy
I will do to your mail such sweetness
I would not like that he never ended

Poem Written in Babel, May 2012

for Rupert Loydell

1.
\def\ProvidesLanguage#1{%
 \begingroup
   \catcode'\10 %
   \@makeother\/%
   \@ifnextchar[%]
     {\@provideslanguage{#1}}

2.
\global\advance\last@language
\ifnum\last@language
\else
 \errmessage{No room for a new\string\language!}
\fi
\global\chardef#1\last@language
\wlog{\string#1 = \string\language\the\last@language}}
   You shouldn't try to proceed from here, type x to quit.}

3.
\ifx\undefined\l@interlingua
 \@nopatterns{Interlingua}
\def\adddialect#1#2{%
\ifx\iflanguage\@undefined
 \input switch.def\relax

4.
\edef\tmp{\string english}
\ifx\languagename\tmp
\else
 \let\l@british\l@UKenglish
\fi
   Maybe you misspelled the language option?}}%
 \fi
\fi

5.
```
\long\def\endotherlanguage{%
  \originalTeX
  \global\ignoretrue\ignorespaces
\PackageError}%
  \bbl\@set@language{#1}}
    {You haven't defined the language #1\space yet}%
{Your command will be ignored, type <return> to proceed}}
```

Sound Poems for Performance with Mick Beck

To You & Me Krakatoa

Anakak! Anakela!
Acaton nokata. Katanowa ka pi.
Orangapulo katanowa.
Ropikela ka! Tapi!

kArtA kArAkA rApUlOrcAttA
OrAngArAkApI tAUkElA
AgArAcAttA kElAtO tAUkElA

Ka! Pi! Katokrak!
Tapikelakato. Kapulalakaton.
Racatta taraka pulautan.
Kapilapippi! Tanpulantaukela!
Ranokata katokrak. Alijar pi kela.
Tajaracatta kelakaga. Okartaka.

AcOnkArAtAkA AlIjArAcAttA
kAtAnOwA rAcAttAnOkAtA
Ana
Anatau
Anatauke
Anataukela
Anataukelaga
Anataukelagapu
Anataukelagapulo
Anataukelagapuloto.
Ananananakakakakak!

*

Horace: Ode 3.30
translated in the manner of Hugo Ball

exegogi ononu onononu
iquedadax altiusquet
quaquaquod

emporu milinnu autetetau
gresti nonannor autetetau
onononu autetetau

ensca
cepsu
citanavita
vivolo
epitalos
exegogi

ededuxi exegogi potenspulor
carcar cadumdau
bitinamimber aquilam
quaquaquod ededuxi

volotam ivervi
cepsu navita
laudicap pyraperen popoten
autetetau nonannor emporu milinnu
posterapossit
autetetau cadumdau autetetau
milinumer auroco
autetetau cadumdau autetetau

exego exegogo exego
iquedadax ononu
altiusquet quaquod

*

Steam at Sheffield
(after Ebenezer Elliott)

   thundever   harmetal   festu   oundark
        issling   graste   wondurm
  redank   kullflam   dremp   murmoke
      storge   smull   acklight
 empless   stoom   hocket   horgerror
     tormspar   oltfire   ipmet
 throom   scrolt   mirachee   terrest
     streeclops   spoud   chimrock
   jull   tamprous   musank   numboom
    afficanal   claffic   empiron
rappling   millity   ratilt   ullroar
     crestu   oltever   neveremp
 thundurge   tamptoil   blackull   skuk
     storror   laborge   chimbrill
  vapling   worstree   uprack   stolt
     streer   esturest   bloopling
 apicease   iproast   volity   fliss
     glight   decloom   umneys
 angream   aloom   crowdense   straste

Lewis & Clark:
An Imaginary Conversation

Scene a tent in the Lost Trail Pass.
L & C evidently exhausted,
drawing exquisite corpses while they
slowly drain their last flask of whisky.

L. Ansisters …
C. Mockersons …
L. Noumerous sperits …
C. Instancetaniously assended …
L. Blounty anamalls …
C. Wrestless deavels …
L. Examoning interals …
C. Flaiming franzey …
L. Prosisely …
C. Smoth jucted pices …
L. Sighns & turrow …
C. Blont selicitations …
L. Murkery debth imigies …
C. Fluctiating intimitions …
L. Parshally intimedate …
C. Fortigueing …
L. Peculial ogressors …
C. Topsaturva …
L. Stold adecrated tropies …
C. Orrigans transfired …
L. Incretiatable farocity …
C. Bearfoot turrouble …
L. Divils repieted excesevely …
C. Sliperery dementions …
L. Tentatious accedents …
C. Naarly supenemary knats …
L. Pustelous ghusts …
C. Musquiters …

L. Musquetoes …
C. Misquetors …
L. Extreen ascid crek …
C. Fraturnal segassity …
L. Deturmind tham suckceed …
C. Soarly chargrined …
L. Disvigored …
C. Ganaraehah …
L. Louis Venerae …
C. Selibrated wrightings vociforate …
L. Inpenetratable outradge laterly luled …
C. Taist graduly provaled …
L. Compessed atmespier …
C. Surpulous froath …
L. Lightineng …
C. Harican padroling surcumfrance …
L. Rugid horozen …
C. Accorgingly steup groround riminds …
L. Pereceived scelestial dungal …
C. Incrediable deabth curioesly scured …
L. Promisquisly delienating heardships …
C. Ferce amcinated moonox gugling …
L. Monsterous diolect …
C. Horriable axcent …
L. Agutation …
C. Understoot …
L. Clift circlier advorsarys inhabid …
C. Gossey virmen atacted …
L. Prosuing curruption …
C. Standart parrilal pinecal …
L. Suffiently defferent deturmonation …
C. Prutty horred errow …
L. Deseption promused inosent …
C. Eturnial voige …
L. Untirely carrestick eydea …
C. Sush homney …
L. Norstrals petially diligient …

C. Axcepting peltry subcistance …
L. Emence rapaid sworms …
C. Imedeatily sorounded …
L. Enjorie ellert …
C. Naucious minets repepeated …
L. Centiring …
C. Waried …
L. Exhosted …
C. Dispear …

The Return of the Logoclast

Safe Passage
(for the last wounded animal in the wood)

'why is reason a voice'
query whether Thomas Wyatt or Judith Goldman
asked me that but at least we're
off on time. 'Hartshorn'
was Byron quoting Pope
you couldn't find a better pair of
wounded animals aboard one ark.
'I' which denotes Byron 'said
<u>all</u> of "<u>us youth</u>" were on a wrong tack'
i.e. 'a wrong revolutionary poetical system'
'But I never said that we did not sail well.'
The Duty Free is now open. Remember that Byron
said this around the time he wrote 'Beppo'
and the voice was reasonably
or not released but he went on saying
very similar things. He's not the only
awkward cuss or the only
one from Cambridge you'll meet on this ferry
although the others claim theirs
is the right revolution
which isn't much of a mutiny
you can either check out the disco
or turn in for the night. Krakatoa's reborn
& growing up fast
there's no lesson in that
re the present condition of English poetry
but best tell the captain
if we're heading that way. The night sea's
so dark the cabin window's a
funny sort of mirror
when I looked I saw
just as two Californian poets
both women

had seemed to predict
for quite different reasons
if that's the right word
Thomas Wyatt. A voice
never hears how it sounds
that's why everyone's in the same boat
there are no degrees of safe passage
the last wounded animal herself doesn't know
her own name or who wrote her

Those Troublesome Disguises
of Jonathan Williams in Bartram's Tree

'sat Will & Kate
    doing a Mr. & Mrs.
Eve & Adam…' –
    another long shot
from the paparazzi?
    A future
Queen of England has tits?
    No
no. It's only that poetical
    chappy & his
missus next door
    via Mr. Gilchrist
via Col. Williams
    'Nobodaddy here
but us'

*

'Maluerne's* ear'

'**spelling according to the*
Rev. Skeats'

[sic]

i.e. when Wm Langland
was the local poet

but in my time
when the Colonel phoned

Malvern

poets Turnbull & Fisher
jumped to it

all ears

*

Tipitiwitchit!

my Gardien Angel's
happy Alacrity

(Mr. Jefferson's
Aphrodite's Mousetrap)
(*Dionaea muscipula*
Venus Flytrap to you)

so we take the Walk
to the very palace garden
of ould Madam flora
the Terrestrial Paradise of Carolina
I die A martar to Botany Gods
climbing trees is over with me in this world

while the exile Kalmia
sings in London

as you are so fond of Mee
tell my Frd J Bartram who sent Mee
to send me Company

*

The student is required
to write a poem
with the following words
in this order

slippelled
crickly
cymophanous
sialagogues
disorb
flacked
adamsite
lick-be-quick
glumes
ineludable
vari-pinct
suasion

& then read
The Lost Lunar Baedeker
again

*

'sorry I'm late'
arriving in the Old Black Lion
in Hay-on-Wye
where the landlord also
jumped to it –

'my mother –'

'Alan'
with what resonance
not quite resignation

'Every Man has a Mother'

*

Colonel

do the digital
signals cross Lethe?

Did you catch that gal
today on Radio 4

'frothing with rage
in Cheriton Fitzpaine'?

Neither philosopher
nor lost lover

she

*

Coda

It seems that O'Nan
hasn't set up a branch
of his Auto Service
in the Trough of Bowland

but you'll find there a sign
flames striped like the Tyger's
with the painted legend
FIRE HAZARD

to which someone has added
with a shaky hand
and a spray can
NO BONKING

Sixty Dyads for David Annwn

man age
since rest
plea sure
for tune
end ears
imp unity
read just
alter native
gene rally
wan ton
heat hen
come dies
sup pose
mist rust
err and
know ledge
person ally
ram page
wake field
hum our
infer no
hot test
his sing
pie ties
best owing
ash ore
tacit urn
be ached
surf ace
or bits
so lid
disc over
amen able
saga city

```
       need led
       rest raining
     thresh old
        pal my
       kind red
      fume scent
      rebel lion
       spar king
       scar let
       torn ado
       pen chant
        nib bled
       rose ate
       page ants
        we stern
        pun gent
       idea lists
       mole sting
       flag rant
       stag nation
      prose cute
        stub born
         is land
         leg ends
       deter mined
        men tally
```

Local Forum

Pond Street Nora could run like stink but
you'd see her sometimes
sat very still on a sack of spuds
then she'd suddenly shout
'is anyone gonna clean these fucking windows'
it was either that or
'You'll not go down Princess Street no more, fucker you'
she had a bad language problem
she reckoned they made tizer from cider and hot water
she liked to recite 'Transport coat religion' and
'you won't get me up them stairs again charlie cooper'
then if anyone laughed at her she'd chant
'Get thee sen a brush and gooen sweep up'
but her favourite was
'fucking well chuck 'em out of West Bar'
she meant the copshop but once
she just kept shouting
'I'll be sat ont fucking saddle'
over and over and another time
'Nar then does thar like potatoes and fish or
fish and potatoes'

Little Herbert was the man in question
Eddie Bedstead collected old wood
Rommel wore welding glasses always
Subway Cyril got the DFC
he used to wear an RAF greatcoat like Tab End Joe
and push a honda placcy everywhere he went
The Green Linnet wore heavy flour make-up
Big Ada packed a punch
she sold fruit and veg
and flowers outside the City Road Cemetery on Sundays
with a turban on her head
Nellie Wellow liked to chop

up her doors and furniture for firewood
The council would replace them
then she'd chop 'em up again
her name may have been Ivy
what an angelic voice

The Duke of Darnall
directed traffic at the end of Change Alley
in his yellow silk gloves and bowler hat
it was a shame he was called Dummy Tailor
it wasn't that he couldn't
he just didn't like talking
he used to live with Russian Edna
who was always in the Barleycorn
she got picked up in the Sportsman
found murdered in High Hazels Park
There were those who said the Duke was to blame
some old lads told me an american soldier
a lorry driver freed after 18 months
said he'd paid her 10 bob
she wasn't worth it and he asked for it back
she'd stuck it up the sleeve of her cardigan
they had a fight and this happened
not in St George's churchyard but
next to the bandstand

On St Martin's Land:
William of Newburgh Annotates
a Poem by J.H. Prynne

a hole in a field
not a well
not a drain
not used by fox
or badger or rabbit
it is always dusk
where the green children live

but when the beans
[broad beans]
were being brought in
pecora patris nostri
in agro pasceremus
[when they were pasturing
their father's cattle]

O
allusive
liminality O
younger cousins
of Gawain's nemesis
Wilkommen!
Aiuto!

Plot Likelihoods

[Score commissioned by Caitlin Buck and Bo Meson for performance at the Sheffield University Festival of the Mind. The text draws on interviews in which six scientists discussed the significance of uncertainty in their disciplines and their allowance for it. The performance took place in St George's Church on 28 September 2012. The musicians were Martin Archer, Mick Beck, Hervé Perez and Johnny Hunter, with Geraldine Monk as 2nd voice.]

V, voice. M, musicians.

1st Movement

V reads solo with marked pauses between lines:

not knowing the answer before you start
to go back through time
I've got a picture here hard to measure
it depends very much on some
badly behaved errors we can't get rid of altogether
you'll find blackbirds you'll find ducks you'll find pigeons
represented visually by bands of uncertainty
numbers the code by which archaeologists
estimate calibration curves
there are only two left in a huge forest
& they never quite reach
I have no choice but to
just because the mound was there
design an experiment to test the hypothesis
do it three times & I'll start to believe it
then take it round to the stats department
to find a set of images of the same object
we can walk down the corridor & tomorrow afternoon
we know people have been living here & there on this axis
20 years 500 years
to get over the significance barrier
to save time & pain

I want you to rest easy
I make a lot of assumptions because
they can sometimes if you're lucky cut a long story short

M respond with lively improvisation which they gradually restrain into a continuous background sound for

2ND MOVEMENT

V reading, with similar line-pauses:

is it really doing what he thinks it's doing
& can he tell you what to do with it
if we built a black hole
what would the experimentalists see
if it wasn't spinning or if it was
uncertainties can vary in size
we've only had one Earth &
there will always be unknowns
let's play & draw cartoons
there's an unpredictability
a trade-off in terms of the scatter
between many assumptions & a few
making simpler or more complicated models

if nanoparticles released by catalytic clothing
do get in the water treatment plant
what will that do to
errors smaller than the points on the graph
you don't know what's going on in between
the first two or three bridges
once you've put some text in
a mathematical forest with ridges in the middle
we can reverse engineer the most likely result
where it's involved in the public realm
to work out how much I trust a singular fit
this particular parameter this inherent instability this

hardest part of the dialogue
the way ocean and climate interact
I would understand as a different simulation
male & female as conflict between pathogen & host
gene sequences long gone
the fibres are thinner than
when I say 'probably' inverted commas
'I tried that & it didn't'
most of us tend to be less explicit about the well-known
meaningless chuck-out of software in error bars
at discrete points from global down to local
it isn't an admission of failure
when you're looking at small changes in the input
variations which tend to be averaged out
solving physical equations of motion in the atmosphere
I wonder what happens if you have evidence for
but can't prove there's a near-identical corridor
in one of its 500,000 iterations produced minutes later
what if I had more money
what if they're frightened by Prince Charles
what if we add this bit of molecule to that

when the benefits outweigh the risks
you can calculate the particles emitted
blackbirds an antler-pick ducks a few pigeons
(remains of)
ensemble predictions
emergent phenotypes in nutshells
what happens first when polymers crystallise
that's a two-way street
an observation orthogonal to current understanding
this field has been in flux for the last 10 years
you have a good feeling but
cannot measure both position & momentum
at the end you can see the prediction's
a highly non-linear model you had to
change to deal with the variation

this wiggly behaviour in the distributions
the stuff has anyway
however fine your dissection of
the degree of interaction between the ice-sheets
(remains of)
you still don't know what's going on inside

Then M again break into lively improvisation which continues through

3rd Movement

in which V improvises text generated from the grids:

A. *V strings these phrases together in a semblance of sense, pausing when a string leads nowhere then trying again to 'fail better':*

just because   they never quite reach   if we built a
    set of images of   your dissection of
simpler or more complicated   error bars   you'll find
    in the middle   thinner than
the code by which   as discrete points from   the significance barrier
    as conflict between   not knowing the
errors smaller than   inverted commas   produced minutes later
    represented visually by   emergent phenotypes
a singular fit   in the distributions   of the scatter
    in flux for the   to be averaged out
depends very much on   the most likely   assumptions because
    if I had more   to go back through
this inherent   you can calculate the   an experiment to test
    what happens first   as a different simulation
less explicit than   what happens if   we can't get rid of
    small changes in   the physical equations of
highly non-linear   calibration curves   can vary in size
    on this axis   (remains of)
it wasn't spinning or   if we add this   at the end you
    have no choice but   do it three times
& it didn't   prove there's a   can he tell you what
    an admission of   the risks

orthogonal to current   where it's involved in   (remains of)
        interaction between   there will always be

B. *in which V is joined by a 2nd voice but neither is foregrounded – these words are just another sound in the mix, delivered in bursts with marked pauses. M play in a similar manner:*

```
curves      deal        work        stuff       still           living
        part        left        answer      bit         last
want        thin        reach       change      start           rest
        picture     back        plant       trust       risks
choice      make        cut         measure     object          set
        time        design      long        handle      can
doing       scatter     see         will        current         size
        ducks       fit         model       text        one
experiment  bands       water       Earth       points          few
        test        low         field       reverse     numbers
bridges     result      walk        host        play            down
        bars        remains     estimate    position    now
lack        ever        know        thematic    miss            here
        rough       taint       part        act         path
main        win         in          each        lay             real
        hang        line        sure        log         rid
imp         on          merge       wing        present         cause
        raw         rust        ratio       mode        pend
gist        sump        thing       inner       not             for
        and         sign        too         stab        one
but         have        moment      till        section         end
        tree        tar         cert        pot         red
if          right       we          get         rest            way
        ridge                   own                     posit
```

C. V's delivery similar to section A while M create rolling waves of sound. 2nd voice initially overlapping with V in duet but perhaps developing a dialogue:

a region inside which   long-chain molecules   how weather will evolve
         a carrier membrane   the physiology that underpins
for instance cloud physics   the trouble is   changes in human dynamics
         the desire for order   back come these
natural systems   catalysts made from titania   whether something is extinct
       if you counted enough   how to interpret
mechanisms by which   over thousands of years   the immune system of
       relaxing the assumption that   defies the way you
but often you can't   from day to day   that flow to perturbations
       look at past environments   how people will react
we all contain carbon   we empirical biologists   need to be clearer
       we do not expect   not because the table
is a midden   sitting in your office   in the sewerage system
       in a research environment   how moisture works inside
a new set of toys   within 10% error   call this Uncertainty Management
       to look at populations   we get some surprises
we will routinely have   it's fine to say   having both is good
       people self-select   without any external field
to measure symmetry   yes it's going to   it switches back for
       appropriately & correctly   of the ocean circulation
20,000 years ago   or one slightly different   can be less demanding
       decorate that with   microbes that clean up

The duet/dialogue stutters to a halt. M gradually restrain improvisation into continuous background sound for

4TH MOVEMENT

although here M are free to improvise response to individual lines, particular words etc – V modulates reading in counter-response, perhaps repeating lines or phrases but maintaining line-pauses as before:

I make a lot of assumptions because
we've only had one Earth
a region inside which you can see some
badly behaved errors we can't get rid of altogether
this particular parameter this inherent instability this
field has been in flux for the last 10 years
it depends very much on some
variations which tend to be averaged out
in one of its 500,000 iterations produced minutes later
you can calculate the particles emitted
you have a good feeling but
however fine your dissection of
a mathematical forest with ridges in the middle
emergent phenotypes in nutshells
a highly non-linear model you had to
design an experiment to test
a set of images of the same object
at discrete points from global down to local
where it's involved in the public realm
I would understand the desire for order
as a different simulation
when you're looking at small changes in the input
but can't prove there's a near-identical corridor
that's a two-way street once you've put
some text into a new set of toys
look at past environments
you can see the prediction's
a trade-off in terms of the scatter
over thousands of years within 10% error
that flow to perturbations
represented visually by bands of uncertainty

making simpler or more complicated models
you don't know what's going on in between
an antler-pick cartoons Prince Charles a few pigeons
(inverted commas) (remains of) (probably)
we know people self-select on this axis
it isn't an admission of failure
when the benefits outweigh the risks
I have no choice but to
work out how much I trust a singular fit
most of us tend to be less explicit about the well-known
errors smaller than the points on the graph
20 years 500 years
between many assumptions and a few

after which M improvise to end.

Idle Time Scans

plateglass plateau
spotlit to split
an absolute alphabet's
foreign fingers

'if I'd brought my compass'

but even if we'd seen
a mormoluche or two
off the coast of Ionia

what then?

*

slave revolts in olden Ataraxia
or that other lost city Eudemonia

happenstop or voicestop
in pretence of anger

'flinging the cartouche to the ground'
(the word was probably 'crutch')

in damned reprehensible
maybe representable domains

whatever this means
'you'll call her Cordelia at least'

*

careless text next carols
careless text next scholars

'he knew how to trifle with the Muses'
but purgative obstacles were yet
another thing he'd forgotten
to make a list of

in an age agog with lowish expectations
barking up the wrong bast or phloem

*

I look at the photo then I
can't remember if I remember
Beulah Spa and the bombed-out
houses around Spa Hill Woods

where a splaying oak from
a Robin Hood book in as I'm
not sure whether when I read
it lately I was reminded
Dick Turpin country

but I was certainly told about
Peter the Hermit
the charcoal burners
and the gibbet which once
stood at Thornton Heath Pond

where they hanged neither Hood
nor Turpin but boys bad as me

*

flutterfights & warsquawks
of magpies & pigeons
claiming the same spacious
limetree branch

predication & prediction
the same root

what it is
to be idly bedevilled by
or else indebted to
an ideal detail

past pests
buoyant as buyouts
purblind & parboiled

'at the end of the day
a rabbit is a rabbit'

was that an explanation
or a conclusion?

*

neither red nor yellow nor purple but
'the dark leathery colour of time'
preserved in the archaeological record
just as it was
in the living rooms of the 1950s
'rooted in relation to
their own set of relatives'
that's something I do remember
Auntie This & Auntie That
the only colourful thing
aunties seemed to have
was a budgie

*

Is your name Croydon?
Tell us what it is like
to be named Croydon.

What difference does it make
whether it means
Crooked or Crocus Valley?

Tell us what it is like
to jump from the upstairs window
of a burning building.

*

a coroner found the first Irish case
of death by spontaneous combustion
on the same day it was announced
that certain neutrinos had been
caught exceeding the speed of light

the coincidence of dates is of no significance
although the first if not the second phenomenon
would have been noted by the uncommercial traveller
I happened to be reading that day

how he met 'a power man on the public Iway'
not a politician but common enough
a century later around South Norwood
or down by the sausage stall at midnight
a tramp everyone believed for reasons
I can't guess a secret millionaire

*

'As two night-birds flit'
'As a shark and dog-fish wait' –

Shelley on Sidmouth & Castlereagh
maybe reminds you of some recent double acts –

the sheer ache of their
haste to chasten –

*

Donna mi priegha
if I've ever heard of
the river Wandle

& because she asks me
I do remember
the trickle of a stream

you could see
at Thornton Heath Rec
through the railings.

Now I read that
Admiral Nelson
did his fishing

in the stretch
which flowed through
Lady Hamilton's garden

she having diverted it
and in his honour
or rather because of

un accidente
ch'é chiamato amore
called it 'the Nile'.

*

When to go flying is only to fall over

To repeat what has been said
in the last person singular or plural
resistance follows reassurance
which then reasserts itself
then there is further resistance & so on

As the psalmist says more than once
Aha

As soon as the calendar's a list
of back-to-back Remembrance Days
the illusion of history will be complete

*

'In the Great Scheme of Things'

'A True & Faithful Relation of
What Passed For'

'One book which is sometimes
referred to as a moveable atlas
had been restored by human beings
page by page'

How distant those days seem.
The chimeras
whether or not they
won that particular war
wrote what nobody would call
an exact account –

& since cameras then offered
a different deception
than ours do
& 'pathos' rhymes with 'photos'
only as 'luckless' with 'knuckles'
& 'cancel' with 'conceal' –

say they wrote what
they never claimed they foresaw

*

You find out about reference
when a word such as 'zeppelin'
conjures the thing up
in your 5-year-old sky. Now

I see it no I didn't. All
I ever saw was the fragment
of one that crash-landed
near my grandpop's house

He made a shineless brooch of it
An exhibit now lost
That tells you everything you
need to know about reference

*

under these 4 umbrellas
there were these 4 poets
one wet August afternoon
walking in Epping Forest
which lays better claim
to Dick Turpin
than Thornton Heath

2 days later
under the same trees
but without umbrellas
there were only 2 poets
picking blackberries
this was just down the road
from High Beach
where the Visitor Centre
records Turpin's pockmarks

but as for a famouser poet
the sales assistant echoes
his own question
John Who?

She didn't need to keep birds: Owls from all over came to call for her birthday

for Geraldine at 60

        strix strix   strix strix
      ninox tyto huhula hoyi
          rufa brama boobook
        ios jubula ketupa
      xenoglaux sceloglaux
   castanops sororcula lempiji
        asio scops   otus siju
  usta pulsatrix alloco
   multipunctata uhu capogrosso
schleiereule harfang
          schneeeule sneewuil
  laponne chevêchette steenuil
    gufo hulotte oehoe
      oeraluil assiolo dwerguil
chico nana barbagianni chivetta
        buho cárabo
uggla tornuggla hornuggla
    effraie chouette
              chat-huant
         hibou lacheule
     buho jubula
  strix strix   strix strix
       ninox
          huhula

The Return of the Logoclast

'Atrocities' I must have misheard
but who was meant by 'Trustees'?
Persons in philosophy
weary as nouns at political half-mast
with their ablatives awry?
The word-happy slapstick scribe
with nothing on his mind
but cosmogony & endtimes
the one whose writing I
keep finding in my notebooks
seems to know all about easy nausea
squalid fugue fog
skewed tobacco toccatas
the tyranny of half rhyme &
wands that do everyday wonders
the catchiest varia of
viral catechisms
trade hidden in an ultradense
triple-dip
circle of icicles
if they can see
it it's not really vacancy
but beast-boats & vision
intimate as antimatter
crumbed in supervision
PLEASE DO NOT POWER OFF
why
    the Manichaeans
didn't for the fun of it
make evil up

LOXHD1

'If gorillas talk to each other
they're keeping it secret'
but there again they kept
themselves secret until 1847

unless we count Hanno's observation
circa 480 BC
of a 'tribe of hairy women'.
'Twenty-five vocalizations are recognized'

at least by us. 'A few individuals
have been taught a subset of sign language'
but as for their
belief in 'spiritual feelings and religious sentiments'

that's not something I'd've said
around 1859 or any time since although
the gene LOXHD1
involved in human hearing and

'therefore thought to be involved in speech
shows just as much
accelerated evolution
in the gorilla'

Complexicon

'This is pointless, Kim.'
'Yes, but it's rather fascinating, isn't it.'
          (*Chase a Crooked Shadow*, 1958)

gallery
allegory
pursed
ellipses
bourgeois
hourglass
deputy
duty
or
import
unity

'Is sign-language
the true language
of Paradise?'
asked Hugo Ball

who may or may
not have foreseen
localised look-alikes
survey monkeys
significant football
etc

'The place which Picabia
assigned to art'
(Richter in retrospect)
'was, so to speak,
a hole in the void'

shared shreds
motormouth martyrs
purest purses
monologuing moonglow
chimes & charms
drifts & figments
ordinary dis
ordered desire

exactly when did I forget
where I found
'A Skreen Full of Puzzles'?

Searching for Sibylla

in the wake of Thomas Lovell Beddoes
and John Cowper Powys

Since notability cannot be established
a species of mantis found in
a large main-belt asteroid
also known as a German poet of the Baroque era
one who foments quarrels
I've talked to a lot of victims of uncommon words

Last house on the left of Blue Ridge, Blue Ridge
the youngest member of the Draconis family
fatal muse of a fragmented Anticyran
her and her witches spitting fire in pine-fir forest
on the one hand and presiding over
the Apollonian oracle at Cumae on the other

sparkling wings unlike most earth fairies
Tyburrina Allumea Queen Consort Squabbler
a duchess a countess a princess
agreeable her discourse and sweet the syllables
so says the Red Book of Hergest
victims of rhyme Di-es ir-ae di-es il-la si-byl-la

Messenger, Singer

the water and the dark material
at Mercury's pole which
Prof. Solomon believes is organic-
rich and my language-imp can't
resist adding in its glory
the signature of hydrogen
delivered by some mixture of
comets and asteroids
of volatile assembly

or as Empedocles I'm also
reminded tonight the first of
December 2012 by the second
set of Ed Dorn's *Songs A Short
Count* said: Love and Strife

A Defence of Poetry

If words & letters
        (chaos chess)
keep jumping about
        (wingless wineglass)
in everybody's minds
        (halcyon balcony)
there will be plagues & earthquakes
        & pornographic pomegranates!
(but you mustn't believe)
        cauliflower camouflage!
(everything litcrit)
        scorpion corpses!
(& health & safety &)
        Prometheus
on the rebound!
        (superstition saith)

Rampant Inertia Revisited:
A Busted Sonnet

milk of amnesia
nonionising
rag life glare
fragile flag
page seepage
unrequited by law
countered terrace
officer gargoyles
greyscale philosophers
cashiered on account
of dataday
rundown rainbows
a tin rib-
boned it-
brain chaos
absorbed in flash crashes
on the nifty fifty
because 'there's only
a certain market
for a certain market'
not so much Caligula
mistaken for a dull
variety of lettuce
as mushroom misnomers
absurd as scented grass
second-guessed
'O yes
the men on the islands
was civil enough'
the cesspool-sewerman
told Mayhew
'they never spoke to us
and we never
spoke to them'

www.ingramcontent.com/pod-product-compliance
Lightning Source LLC
Chambersburg PA
CBHW031157160426
43193CB00008B/400